WILDLIFE

WILDLIFE

Joyce Robins

||| •PARRAGON• |||

Acknowledgements

Bruce Coleman Ltd/Jen & Des Bartlett page 10; /**Erwin & Peggy Bauer** pages 14, 21, 60, 64; /**R.I.M. Campbell** pages 24, 68; /**John Cancalosi** pages 28, 71; /**Alain Compost** page 23; /**Peter Davey** pages 22, 40–1; /**Jeff Foott Productions** page 39; /**Francisco Futil** page 13; /**Johnny Johnson** page 11; /**Janos Jurka** page 53; /**D.J.C. Klees** page 76; /**Stephen J. Krasemann** pages 9, 36; /**Wayne Lankinen** page 50; /**Werner Layer** page 35; /**L.C. Marigo** page 31; /**Rinie van Meurs** page 47; /**Goetz D. Plage** page 32; /**Eckart Pott** page 66; /**Hans Reinhard** cover, pages 6, 15, 42, 45, 48, 56, 57, 59, 62, 63, 77; /**John Shaw** page 16; /**Sullivan & Rogers** page 18; /**Jan Taylor** page 67; /**Kim Taylor** page 8; /**Rod Williams** pages 25, 26, 75; /**Konrad Wothe** pages 34, 54, 70.

The Image Bank/Joseph Van Os page 29.

Natural History Photographic Agency/Gerard Lacz page 27; /**Otto Rogge** page 17.

Oxford Scientific Films/Tom J. Ulrich page 37.

Planet Earth Pictures/Richard Coomber page 72–3; /**David J. McChesney** page 65; /**Peter Scoones** page 46.

Robert Harding Picture Library/T.D. Winter page 51.

First published in Great Britain in 1994 by
Parragon Book Service Ltd
Units 13–17, Avonbridge Trading Estate
Atlantic Road, Avonmouth
Bristol BS11 9QD

Publishing Manager: Sally Harper
Editor: Michele Staple
Design: Robert Mathias/Helen Mathias

ISBN 1 85813 856 6

Printed in Italy

Contents

CHAPTER ONE

Grasslands and Prairies

Grasslands, where rainfall is limited so that only grasses, low bushes and a few hardy trees can survive, account for over a quarter of the earth's surface. The grasses provide food for grazing animals and they, in turn, provide food for the carnivores who prey on them. The largest remaining natural grassland is the African savannah, much of it protected in large reserves where, at the beginning of the dry season, vast herds gather to make long journeys in search of fresh grass and water.

The elephant, the giant of the grasslands, needs 150 kg (330 lb) of food a day and has to spend up to sixteen hours out of twenty-four collecting enough to survive. The bulk of its diet is grass but it will also bulldoze whole trees, eating the leaves and stripping off branches and bark to get to the succulent layers beneath. It walks slowly – usually at about 8 km (5 miles) an hour – and silently, on flat feet thickly cushioned so that they can adapt to differences in terrain and comfortably support a 4 – 6-tonne weight.

Useful tools

Unlike most grass-eaters the elephant does not need to bend down to graze; it simply lowers its trunk, tests the food, then transfers it to the mouth for chewing. Its trunk is an amazingly versatile tool, acting as arm, hand, nose and water siphon into the bargain. It can suck up 9 l (2.5 gallons) of water at a time, either for drinking or for spraying as a shower

FACING PAGE: *Elephants live in co-operative communities of up to fifty animals, made up of several family units.*

LEFT: *Surprisingly, giraffes have the same number of bones in their necks as humans, but they are much more spread out.*

bath. At other times the trunk is used for a dust bath, to protect the animal from sunburn. The elephant's sense of smell is highly developed; if it senses danger it will raise its trunk to sniff the air, and it can also be used to locate water beneath the surface. The trunk is both strong and extraordinarily sensitive, being able to lift obstacles from the elephant's path and pick berries using its manipulative tip without squashing them.

The elephant's name comes from the Hebrew word for ivory and its tusks are elongated incisors growing from the upper jaw. In an adult male, these can weigh up to 40 kg (90 lb) each but unfortunately, the more magnificent the tusks, the more likely the elephant is to fall victim to poachers, who can command a high price for ivory. The tusks can be formidable weapons but are more often used to intimidate an enemy, to dig a pit or uproot a tree. An elephant is normally right- or left-tusked, just as humans are right or left-handed, so one tusk wears down more quickly than the other. The loss of one or more tusks in an accident or a fight can have a profound effect on the animal's temperament.

Elephants live in herds of up to fifty

made up of several family units, and this results in a very co-operative, caring community. When a baby is born, the mother is assisted by a young male and an elderly female, probably both members of her family, and the rest of the group form a circle round them, facing outwards to ensure their safety. Once the infant arrives they all gather to inspect it with their trunks. If a baby is orphaned, it will be adopted by another mother and treated as her own. When a member of the herd falls ill, other elephants will prop up their sick relative between them so that it will not fall and crush its lungs. When one of their number is dying, they will stay beside it and comfort it with the touch of their trunks.

Like the elephant, the giraffe is uniquely adapted to suit its environment; it has evolved long legs, a long neck and a long prehensile tongue. Though it has the same number of bones in its neck as humans, they are elongated so that it can browse on the top leaves of the acacia tree, plucking them with its 40-cm (16-in) tongue. The top leaves receive most sunlight so give the best nutrition, and in times of drought the giraffe often fares better than other herbivores. It is the

RIGHT: *Known as the 'giraffe-necked gazelle', the gerenuk excels at reaching high-growing leaves.*

ABOVE: *To elude predators, springboks flee in a series of high, bouncing leaps that confuse their attackers.*

FACING PAGE: *This Burchell's zebra may seem too flamboyant to miss, but its stripes provide surprisingly good camouflage.*

necks from side to side, butting each other's heads with their bony, skin-covered horns. They do not use their damaging hooves and seldom inflict permanent injury.

Self-preservation

The giraffe's height enables it to watch for predators many kilometres away and several animals browsing together will usually face in different directions to keep a thorough lookout. Giraffes are often seen with large crowds of antelopes and zebras, especially at water holes, for the greater the number of animals gathering together, the better their chances are of sensing danger. The only antelope which rivals the giraffe in the search for high-growing food is the gerunuk, which is also partial to acacia leaves. It is known as the 'giraffe-necked gazelle' because it can reach 2 m (6 ft) into the tree by standing on its hind legs, balancing against a branch with its front hooves and reaching up to the leaves with its long neck.

Antelopes have their own ways of responding to danger. The large heavy elands, travelling in single file in herds of up to a hundred, are warned by barks

world's tallest animal, standing up to 5.5 m (18 ft) tall, and has a special grace as it ambles along, moving two legs on one side of its body simultaneously, then moving the other two.

Though they live in herds, giraffes are not as family-oriented as elephants. The young often seem to be left to their own devices for long periods and the make-up of the herd is constantly changing, which leads to frequent squabbles over leadership. When two males decide to challenge each other for supremacy, they stand with their feet wide apart and swing their

from the males and take flight at up to 64 km/h (40 mph), the males bringing up the rear for protection. The springboks, the national emblem of South Africa, stand less than 1 m (3 ft) high, but when frightened they leap 4 m (13 ft) into the air in a horseshoe shape, head down and the crest of white hairs along the back raised to signal to other animals that something is amiss. The impalas, the most graceful of antelopes, keep a watchful eye for enemies as they graze in their herds and, at the first sign of any threat, they scatter, leaping in all directions to confuse the hopeful predator.

Zebras rely on keen eyesight, a good sense of smell and fleetness of foot to escape from danger. Though they are often referred to as horses with stripes, zebras, with their long ears and short stiff manes, are more like asses. Normally they are peaceful animals, but they do have a vicious kick. The most common species is Burchell's zebra, which has stripes that reach under the belly and form a Y-shaped pattern across the rump, and the tallest is Grevy's zebra, with narrow and closer stripes which do not continue on the underside. But whatever the species, no two animals are identically marked.

Several theories have been put forward to explain why the zebra bears stripes: they may provide good camouflage for the half-light when predators are at their most active or they may serve to dazzle and disorient an assailant. On the other hand, they may be designed to identify individual zebras. The pattern of stripes varies most noticeably across the rump and such an obvious means of recognition can be very useful in keeping the herd together as it flees at top speed.

Baboons often form an alliance with antelopes, particularly the impala, to defeat the common enemy. The baboon acting as lookout in a tree may spot the predator first, or the impala may scent it; either way they warn one another. The baboons also use other animals as 'danger scouts' at the water hole, watching while giraffes, zebras and gazelles gather, relying on them to scent danger, then as they leave moving in cautiously for a hasty drink. The society of these ground-living monkeys is strictly hierarchical, with a troop of forty or so ruled by a group of dominant males, who have first pick of females and food.

Baboons have to spend most of the day foraging for food, and when they set forth, they walk in ordered formation: in front are the strongest of the young males, with other young males guarding the flanks and the rear. Females without babies and the lower-status members of the society come next, then at the centre of the group are the dominant males, forming a protective ring around the mothers with babies clinging under their bodies.

Grassland predators

The lion is the largest carnivore of the African savannah, feeding mainly on zebra, wildebeest, antelope and buffalo. A male can weigh 227 kg (500 lb) and stand 1 m (3 ft) at the shoulder but he is too cumbersome and with the great ruff around his neck, too noticeable to make a successful predator. Consequently, it is the more streamlined female who does most of the hunting. Unlike other cats, lions are not solitary. They live in groups, greeting one another by rubbing faces or

RIGHT: *A group of baboons will often turn and confront a predator if they feel that they have a good chance of victory.*

licking one another's heads and sleeping close together, their bodies often touching. Lionesses will 'mind' the cubs of other females who are out hunting. They hunt in a group too, which makes sense for an animal that cannot run as fast as most of its prey. Several lions can encircle a herd to prevent escape, then pick off an animal each, or they can bring down a larger creature such as a giraffe or a buffalo by working as a team. After a kill the males eat first, then the females, and lastly the cubs. The most aggressive, pushy cubs will fare best and if food is very scarce, some cubs may starve. On the whole, lions are lazy animals who spend eighteen or twenty hours a day resting and will steal the kill of another creature, such as the hyena, whenever they get the chance.

In contrast, the cheetah is the fastest animal on four legs ever known. Its long body is lighter and slimmer than the other big cats, and its spine is more flexible. Its blunt claws are only half retractable, so that they act in the same way as spikes on running shoes. A cheetah at full speed can reach 100 km/h (62 mph). It sleeps at night and hunts in the early morning and late afternoon so as to

ABOVE: *Lion cubs are cared for by the whole pride, with lionesses 'minding' the cubs of other females while they are hunting.*

FACING PAGE: *The cheetah reaches its top speed of 100 km/h (62 mph) from a standing start in only three seconds.*

follow their mother on the hunt from an early age, and when there is a kill they eat immediately, unlike lion cubs, who have to wait their turn.

The serval, one of the smaller cats, also depends on speed, being able to run fast enough to catch a bird on the wing. Its fawn coat with black spots provides good camouflage and its long legs enable it to peer over tall grasses to sight its prey, which it then pursues in a series of long leaps. It uses its excellent hearing to detect one of its favourite meals, the mole rat, burrowing underground.

Below ground

avoid direct competition with the lion, and its methods are completely different. The cheetah runs down its prey, depending on speed for its final dash, and if it does not catch up within 400 m (437 yd) or so, it gives up and goes in search of another quarry. It brings down the prey by swiping at its back legs, and then fastens its jaws on the throat long enough to suffocate it. Its hunting is most successful in areas where the grass is not too tall, so that it can reach its full speed. Cubs

The mole rat is just one of the burrowing creatures who make their homes below the grasslands of the world. Found mainly in Africa, but also in Russia and the Middle East, it has silky, chestnut-coloured fur and measures about 23 cm (9 in). Though it sometimes comes to the surface after dark, it lives mainly underground, feeding on roots and bulbs, and its eyes have almost disappeared.

The grassy steppes of eastern Europe and western Asia are the home of the common hamster. This fastidious little creature digs to a depth of 38–76 cm (15–30 in) and hollows out a central chamber leading to several smaller chambers for resting, excretion, food storage and so on. Its winter burrow will have separate compartments for each type of food. In summer it comes out at night to find food, which it stores in cheek pouches, and in winter it goes into semi-hibernation, waking from time to time to feed. The golden hamster, which has become popular as a pet, is a different species, descended from a litter found in Syria in 1930.

The prairie dogs, the burrowing squirrels of the North American prairies, have a more extensive system of underground tunnels. Each burrow has a main shaft with numerous horizontal branches leading off it, one for each of up to 15 members of a group. The burrows link up so that members of different groups can visit one another and a prairie dog 'town' can cover over 50 ha (123 acres). Once, before settlers ploughed up the land and deprived the animals of their habitat, a town could stretch over 100 km (62 miles). Each burrow is surrounded by a conical mound of earth to prevent flooding and one member of the group keeps

ABOVE: *The prairie dogs of the United States build the animal world's largest colonies, which may be inhabited by millions of animals.*

watch from the mound, barking a warning when it spots an enemy (it is because of this barking that the prairie dog gets its name). Unlike hamsters, prairie dogs do not store food and when the cold weather comes, they sleep until it is over.

The wombat makes its underground home in the dry open country of central and southern Australia, digging deep burrows up to 30 m (100 ft) long. It eats grasses and tree roots and sleeps through the day in its comfortable, grass-lined nest chamber. It can go without water for months on end, extracting the moisture it needs from its food. Wombats are solitary creatures who meet only to mate. The females give birth to a single baby which they carry in a rear-facing pouch for six or seven months.

Down under

The best-known of today's marsupials is the kangaroo. Although marsupials (mammals which carry their young in pouches) were common in the days of the dinosaurs, they only survived in Australia, where it is possible to find marsupial mice, rats, moles and squirrels. Because marsupial babies are only partly formed when they are born, they need their pouch time to develop sufficiently before they can take their place in the world. Though the adult kangaroo stands at 1.8 m (6 ft) and weighs 90 kg (200 lb), the little joey measures only 2.5 cm (1 in) long. It spends about five months in the mother's pouch feeding on her milk and occasionally sampling grass by sticking out its head while the mother is grazing.

The kangaroo is built to travel long distances in an energy-efficient manner, using its hind legs as springs. It can bound along at 48 km/h (30 mph) over short distances covering 4.5–10 metres (15–33 ft) in one jump. When grazing it walks on all four feet, and when sitting it rests on its huge back feet, using its thick tail for extra support. It usually lies down to rest on its stomach, with its back legs on either side and its front legs together, so that it can be ready to leap up in a moment; only when it is confident of its safety will it lie on its side. The powerful back feet, equipped with sharp claws, are not only used for travel but also as defensive weapons, being capable of inflicting much damage as they are lashed out.

Another strange creature of the Australian plains is the emu, the flightless bird which can stand up to 2 m (6.5 ft) tall. It is well adapted to its environment with a double layer of feathers to protect it from the heat, long legs and short toes for energy-saving long-distance walking, and a light body with mostly hollow bones. Usually it moves slowly but, when necessary, it can run at nearly 50 km/h (30 mph).

It is the male emu who builds the nest and once the female has laid the eggs – up to sixteen of them, each weighing up to 500 g (1 lb) – her job is done. It is the male who sits on the eggs for the next eight weeks to incubate them. During this time he will seldom eat or drink and will lose about 8 kg (18 lb) in weight. After the chicks are born, he will look after them for the next eighteen months, teaching them the skills they need to survive.

RIGHT: *A kangaroo spends the first five months of its life in its mother's pouch, feeding on her milk and the occasional nibble of grass.*

CHAPTER TWO

The Tropical Rainforest

The enormous trees of the rainforest stretch skywards, their top foliage overlapping to form a thick canopy, which allows little light to penetrate to the ground beneath. The hot, humid climate has changed little in 60 million years, providing an environment that fulfils the basic needs of animals (food, moisture and warmth) in abundance. Although visitors to the rainforest might be disappointed to catch only a few glimpses of animal life, they would hear it all around as unseen creatures crashed through the branches and the cries of birds and monkeys echoed through the foliage by day and night.

In the jungles of South America – which account for half of all the world's moist tropical rainforest – the monkey population is extensive and varied but the noisiest of them all are the howler monkeys. Starting the day with a great raucous chorus, their powerful voices carry for many kilometres. Throughout the day they will howl to warn others off their territory and if two troops meet they howl loud and long at one another until one troop backs off. Howlers are not very adventurous, keeping to a well-defined territory and seldom venturing down to the ground, not even to drink. Their diet of fruit and leaves keeps them supplied with all the moisture they need.

The fifth limb

Like the other 'New World' monkeys of South America, howlers have long, pre-

FACING PAGE: *The booming calls of howler monkeys can carry for many kilometres through the dense foliage of the rainforest.*

hensile tails which they use as a fifth limb, hanging from it or wrapping it round branches to steady themselves or to prevent themselves from falling while they sleep. These tails are so sensitive that they can pick up small objects, and some New World monkeys can be seen caressing one another with the tips of their tails. Howlers are infrequent jumpers, preferring to make slower progress by climbing across adjoining branches, unlike spider monkeys, the acrobats of the forest. These are slender, wiry animals who most resemble spiders when they hang by their tails, with all limbs free for fruit gathering. They live high in the trees in troops numbering up to fifty, and though they split into smaller groups during the day, they never wander far and will immediately band together when a special call warns them of danger. They threaten intruders by throwing twigs and branches at them.

Squirrel monkeys are some of the prettiest and smallest of the South American monkeys, measuring only 25 cm (10 in), with large heads and greeny-grey fur. They prefer to feed on eggs and insects and usually make their homes on the edge of the forest. They are easily tamed

and, like the woolly monkeys, whose grey or brown woolly coats make them look particularly appealing, they are often kept locally as pets. Sadly this usually involves killing the mothers in order to rob them of their young. Capuchins, too, make popular pets and in Europe they were familiar to past generations as the organ-grinders' monkeys. They are clever and cunning, quick to imitate anything they are shown and, even in the wild, able to use a stone as a tool to crack nuts.

Quarrelsome but cheerful

The 'Old World' monkeys of Africa and Asia are generally more aggressive and quarrelsome than their New World relatives but they also have more lively and cheerful dispositions. They lack the advantage of the strong, prehensile tail but often have useful cheek pouches in which to store their food. The colobus monkeys are shy and timid, adept at hiding by remaining motionless among dense foliage, and take refuge in the tree-tops at night. They always seem to be on the move, staying in small family groups ruled by an elderly male, and shrieking at any intruders who stray into their territory. As they do not need to descend to the forest floor they avoid many animal predators, but in the past they were shot in their thousands for their long, silky pelts, which were made into ceremonial tribal cloaks in Africa and coats in Europe.

Monkeys who live on the forest floor nccd to be bolder and more bellicose than their tree-dwelling cousins. Male mandrills, for example, with their powerful bodies and well-developed canine teeth, can deal easily with most predators and will even see off a hungry leopard. They are striking dark brown creatures, with a ring of white bristles round the face, an orange-yellow beard, and vivid red and blue markings on both face and hindquarters. Their distinctive colours deepen when the mandrill becomes angry and serve to intimidate both predators and younger male mandrills who have not yet developed their mature markings. Mandrills live in large family groups, which can number as many as

RIGHT: *Distinguished by their long, flowing coats, colobus monkeys are timid creatures, adept at hiding in dense foliage.*

ABOVE: *The chimpanzee enjoys the company of its own kind, living in family groups of up to eighty.*

200. They are highly organized with a strict hierarchy, and the males guard their mates jealously.

Intelligent apes

Apes are larger and more intelligent than monkeys, with arms that are long in proportion to their bodies and without tails. Gorillas can stand 1.8 m (6 ft) tall and weigh 200 kg (440 lb) but, in spite of their massive and robust frames, they are peaceable animals who seldom get involved in disputes between themselves and would never attack without provocation. They are probably as intelligent as chimpanzees, who are the most 'human' of the apes, but do not have their curiosity or persistence. Even in the wild, chimpanzees have worked out how to use simple tools: they use sticks to poke their way into termites' nests when they want a tasty snack, and pads of leaves to soak up water from the hollows of trees when they are thirsty. In captivity, they quickly learn to solve problems and imitate humans. They can move quite fast by swinging through the trees but whether they spend more time on the ground or aloft through the trees depends on the amount of food available and the number of predators in the area. Seven or eight hours a day are spent gathering food, which is done with plenty of noise, and much of the remainder of the daylight hours is spent grooming one another. At night they build nests in the trees, twisting branches to form a platform and covering themselves with leaves to keep themselves warm.

Both gorillas and chimpanzees are found in Africa, but the other apes – the gibbons and orang-utans – make their home in the tropical forests of Asia. The gibbons are slender and swift tree-dwellers, swinging athletically from branch to branch and capable of 9-m (30-ft) leaps, but when on the ground they are the only apes who always stand or walk upright. The orange-brown orang-utan, whose name means 'man of the forest', is too heavy for the high life of the trees but is a good climber nonetheless, preferring to inhabit the middle storeys. Its arms are one-and-a-half times as long

FACING PAGE: *Unlike many apes, the male orang-utan is a loner, mixing with others only for breeding purposes.*

Left: Bush babies come out at night to feed on insects, flowers, fruit and birds' eggs.

as its legs and it uses its hands and feet with equal dexterity. Like the chimpanzee, it builds a nest at night, but whereas the chimp is a gregarious animal, with a family group of up to eighty, the male orang-utan is a solitary creature who mixes with others only during the mating season.

Night and day

African bushbabies and pottos belong to the same order of mammals as monkeys and apes. Bushbabies, so-called because of their distinctive cry that sounds like a wailing baby, are also often known as 'night apes'. They are appealing animals, with long silky fur, large eyes and bushy tails, and their great leaps – they can jump as far as 4.5 m (15 ft) – are possible because their hind legs are longer than their front ones. They spend their days sleeping, well hidden in tree foliage or abandoned birds' nests, and come out at night to feed. The ends of their toes and fingers are flattened into thick pads of skin to enable them to grip the trunks of trees, and they have an odd habit of frequently licking their hands and feet, or even urinating on them. Scientists disagree as to whether this is to improve their grip or to leave their smell as a territorial marker.

Like bushbabies, pottos have the huge eyes of the nocturnal hunter and they too sleep through the day, curled up in tree hollows with their heads buried in their arms. They move slowly and do not attempt to jump, relying on stealth to catch their prey. They creep up quietly on insects, snails and fledgling birds, seizing them quickly with their hands. Their only defence against their own predators is to curl into a ball and stay absolutely still.

The super-intelligent coati of the racoon family is a versatile and active hunter, climbing trees to catch birds and lizards, and killing frogs and rodents on the ground, though it is just as happy to eat ripe fruit. It locates its food by smell, grubbing for insects with its long, pointed muzzle. The female and young animals travel in groups of up to twenty, preferring to hunt at dawn and dusk to avoid the heat of the day. A male will only join the group in the mating season. Coati have long grey or chestnut brown bodies and striped tails, which they hold upright.

ABOVE: *Travelling in groups of up to twenty, coatis hold their ringed tails high as a signal to the rest of the group.*

ABOVE: *A nocturnal animal, the kinkajou is also called the 'honey bear' because of its fondness for honey.*

Seldom seen

Several of the inhabitants of the tropical forests are shy and seldom seen, taking advantage of the dense vegetation to hide themselves away. The kinkajou only comes out at night and so little is known of its habits. Some scientists claim that it is vegetarian while others insist that it eats birds, insects and small mammals. Its fondness for honey, together with its soft woolly fur, has led to it often being called the 'honey bear'. It is well adapted to life in the trees, with its front legs shorter than its hind legs and its long, prehensile tail, which the young kinkajou uses to hang from a branch by the time it is a few weeks old. As such a tail would be very unusual for a carnivore, this may be the clue to its diet.

The bongo and the okapi, the only true browsing mammals of the tropical forests, are both secretive and reclusive, the bongo so much so that it has only rarely been glimpsed by non-forest dwellers. This forest-dwelling antelope has a red-brown coat with narrow white lines running across its back. Both sexes have horns shaped like lyres which are up to 1 m (3 ft) long. It clings to dense patches of forest, only venturing out at night in pairs or small groups to search for choice shoots and plants. The okapi, on the other hand, is a solitary creature, which was only 'discovered' and named as recently as 1900. A relative of the giraffe, though without its length of neck, it can reach up to 3 m (10 ft) in the trees, helped by its 35-cm (14-in) tongue. Though it looks something like a giraffe, it is about the size of a horse with a deep chestnut-brown coat, marked on the upper parts of its legs with zebra-like black-and-white stripes. The male bears short horns on the forehead. A favourite dinner dish of the pygmies, its acute sense of hearing helps it to avoid humans and also its great enemy, the leopard.

The big cats

The leopard is, without doubt, one of the most beautiful of the jungle cats. Its spotted coat provides perfect camouflage in the light and shadow of the forest foliage, rendering it almost invisible when lying along the branch of a tree or prowling through the undergrowth. However, the leopard will also adapt to other habitats and, besides the forest, can make its

RIGHT: *The okapi relies on its keen sense of hearing to help it elude its predators, which include leopards and humans.*

ABOVE: *The jaguar is a powerful hunter, relying on stealth to take its prey unawares.*

much as 112 kg (247 lb). If the prey is large the leopard will usually take it up into a tree and drape it over a branch to keep it safe from poachers; it can then return for several days to eat from it. It is such a clean and fastidious eater that when it has finished all that is left is a skin, hanging from the branch.

The largest of the American cats is the jaguar, looking rather like a heavily built leopard and just as adaptable. Its name comes from an Indian word *yaguara* meaning 'he who kills with one leap', and it is a fearsome hunter, either slinking up on its prey until it is within striking distance and then leaping on it, or waiting silently on a branch over a river or pool and dropping down on an unsuspecting drinker. It is a strong swimmer and is at ease in the water; when the rivers are swollen and turbulent in heavy floods, the jaguar can be seen floating along peacefully on a log. It is such a successful hunter that local tribespeople believe it can hypnotize its quarry into standing still and waiting for the killing bite, but there is little evidence to support this. Sometimes the tables are turned and a herd of peccary will corner and kill their predatory enemy. As well as hunting pec-

home in the savannah or the mountains and thrive in close proximity to people. It is particularly fond of dog and will put aside its normal caution to raid a village for a tasty meal. It hunts at night, stalking its quarry with great stealth, its sensitive hearing tuned to pick up the slightest sound. It preys on monkey, forest antelope, wild pig, birds and reptiles and has been known to kill animals weighing as

caries, deer, tapirs, monkeys and birds, the jaguar will scoop the body of a turtle out of its shell without breaking it and catch fish by flipping them out of the water with a huge paw. Local Indians claim that it first attracts the fish by flicking its tail up and down in the water but experts dispute this, although their knowledge of this reclusive animal is far from complete.

In spite of the magnificent tiger's reputation for attacking humans, it much prefers to give them a wide berth. When a human is assailed by a tiger, it usually turns out to be an old or injured animal, no longer swift enough to catch its natural prey. It haunts the thickest, shadiest and swampiest parts of the forest, lying in wait for its prey beside rivers or alongside recognized paths to watering places. If the kill is too large to devour on the spot, the tiger will drop it into a thicket and stay with it for several days, eating frequent meals and not being deterred when the meat goes 'off'. It is a poor climber built for stalking prey rather than chasing it at speed, so the tiger has to work hard for its food: perhaps only one attack in twenty results in a kill.

Tigers probably originated from

Siberia and, as naturally northern animals, they dislike intense heat, preferring to spend the hottest time of the day resting in the deepest shade they can find, or even immersing their bodies in shallow water to keep cool. They spend more than three-quarters of the day resting and give themselves a thorough grooming morning and evening, using the same technique as the domestic cat. They usu-

ABOVE: *During the heat of the day, tigers will lie in deep shade, or immerse themselves in shallow water.*

ally hunt at night, though this preference may have developed out of a need to keep well away from human hunters. Those that have lived for some years in reserves without fear from hunters are more likely to hunt at any time when easy prey is available.

Birds of the forest

The constant chatter of birds and flashes of their splendid plumage add noise and colour to the dark rainforest. Some of the best known are the gaudy macaws, the largest members of the parrot family: the scarlet macaw with its bright red body and yellow-and-blue wings, the gold-and-blue macaw, and the military macaw, with its brilliant greeny-blue plumage. Two of the macaw's four toes point backwards for extra grip, and it uses its hooked bill, which is strong enough to crack nuts, as an extra climbing aid. It is a sociable bird, flying about in flocks, incessantly twittering and shrieking.

The toucan is just as gregarious, living in a noisy group of a dozen or more birds, and spending all its time in the trees. It nests in tree hollows all year round, with several birds roosting together. Its brightly coloured serrated bill is often as long as its body, but in spite of this impressive size it is quite light in weight, as the inside is a honeycomb of fibres filled with air. The colours of the bill serve to attract a mate and to intimidate its enemies, but naturalists have been unable to find a scientific explanation for its size. It is useful for picking fruit growing on branches that would not support the toucan's weight, but the bird then has to tilt its head right back in order to swallow.

The smallest bird in the world is the vivid bee hummingbird, measuring as little as 5 cm (2 in). Its tiny feet hardly allow it to walk or climb, and its wings beat so fast as it hovers over a flower – up to 80 beats per second – that they make the humming sound which has given the bird its name. The jewel-like creature can visit many flowers in a very short time, flitting busily from bloom to bloom and efficiently sucking up nectar with its slender, pointed bill and cylindrical tongue. It has remarkable stamina and speed, flying at up to 96 km/h (60 mph), and is surprisingly aggressive, being able to drive off much larger birds.

The hoatzin, most often found along

the rivers of the Amazon basin, is one of the strangest of the jungle birds. It is about the size of a crow with yellowy-brown plumage, red eyes, and a crest resembling that of a peacock on a tiny head. It resides in colonies in a nest consisting of an untidy pile of sticks. When the baby hoatzin is born it is equipped with claws at the edges of its wings and this strange feature links it with the world's first known bird, the extinct Archaeopteryx. The young bird uses these claws to scramble about in the trees when it leaves the nest, but as it matures and learns to fly, these disappear. If danger threatens the baby hoatzin, it will dive straight into the river and stay there until all is safe, whereupon it will scramble back up to the nest. Because hoatzin smell rather like crocodiles and their cry sounds like that of a reptile, so they are often called the 'reptile birds'.

ABOVE: *The bright colours of the toucan's beak serve to frighten off predators, such as hawks.*

CHAPTER THREE

The Great Deserts

Most of the world's great deserts lie along belts of high atmospheric pressure near the equator and they extend over vast amounts of land: the Sahara alone covers more than 9 million square kilometres (3.5 million square miles). Deserts are arid lands which receive less than 25 cm (10 in) of rain a year, usually in sudden, short storms, and in some deserts no rain falls for years on end. The popular idea of the desert is a land of rolling sand dunes, whipped into peaks and troughs by the wind, but this only accounts for a small part of the picture: more often deserts are empty plains of gravel or flat stony ground with a smattering of scrub vegetation.

In the hot deserts the temperature rises quickly during the day so that by noon it may be 50°C (122°F), then at night it drops dramatically to near freezing. A surprising number of creatures manage to live in these harsh conditions, sheltering during the heat of the day, so that the desert seems empty and lifeless, and only emerging to go about their business at night.

The gerbil of Africa, the kangaroo rat of North and Central America and the jerboa of Asia are all desert dwellers with a good deal in common: they need little or no water and they have long hind feet for jumping, so that they do not need to come into constant contact with the hot ground. They also have long tails which help with balance when they jump and support when they sit upright. The jerboa, which resembles a tiny kangaroo,

FACING PAGE: *Seed-eaters such as the gerbil conserve the water they gain from their food by passing very little urine.*

ABOVE: *Jerboas deal with the extreme dryness of the desert by slowing down their metabolism for a few days at a time.*

FACING PAGE: *The enormous ears of the fennec fox act as a cooling system; heat escapes easily through their large surface area.*

Keeping cool

The little fennec fox and the jackrabbit are both highly specialized animals, whose bodies are supremely adapted to desert life. Both have huge ears which act as cooling systems, the blood vessels on the large, thin surface allowing heat to escape. Animals living in cold climates usually have small ears, to conserve heat. The fennec fox is the smallest member of the fox family, its body measuring 41 cm (16 in) or less, but its ears can be up to 15 cm (6 in) long. Not only do these large ears help regulate its temperature but they also enable it to hear the slightest sound made by the lizards and locusts on which it preys. It is a sociable animal, living in small groups, and like many desert creatures it burrows in the sand during the day and becomes active at night, moving across the sand on hairy soles. The jackrabbit – which is really a hare rather than a rabbit – is slightly larger, its body measuring up to 53 cm (21 in), and its ears up to 20 cm (8 in). If its sensitive hearing alerts it to danger, it can bound off across the desert at 70 km/h (43 mph).

Yet another burrowing animal is the hides from heat in its burrow and escapes quickly from its enemies by bounds of up to 2.5 m (8 ft). The kangaroo rat has roomy cheek pouches to enable it to carry food back to the burrow, and the mouse-like gerbil also hoards large amounts of food against lean times. Known as sand rats, gerbils obtain all the moisture they need from the night-time dew on their food, so that they never need to drink.

ABOVE: *The jackrabbit's enormous ears serve two purposes – they give it acute hearing, and help regulate its temperature.*

ably accurate at hitting its target at distances of up to 3 m (12 ft) and the liquid can cause temporary blindness, so predators soon learn to be wary.

The tortoise can withdraw for safety into its rigid carapace, or shell, which is a shield of bony plates to prevent predators from getting at its soft body. It can go for long periods without food and water and because it moves so slowly it uses up very little energy. The leathery skin of its head and limbs reduces moisture loss as well as protecting it from sharp stones and spiky desert plants as it lumbers along. The female tortoise simply lays her eggs in the sand but does not incubate them, relying on natural heat to hatch them.

Survival strategies

spotted skunk, a slow mover who spends most of the day underground, emerging in the cool of the night to forage for insects, small animals and fruit. As it is not fleet of foot, it has another method of self-protection. First it stands on its hands to display its black-and-white markings, but if this is not enough to scare its enemy, it squirts a smelly liquid from scent glands under its tail. It is remark-

The tiny creatures of the desert have developed their own survival strategies. In the Namib Desert of south-west Africa, there may be 1.3 cm (0.5 in) of rainfall a year or there may be no rain at all, but a dawn fog instead, caused by the Arctic current in the Atlantic Ocean, which penetrates far inland and causes a heavy dew. This dew gives the local beetles all the moisture they need. One species makes long channels in the sand before the dew arrives, then journeys back through the channels, absorbing water from the wet sand. Another stands still to allow the dew to condense on its back. It then stands on the crest of a sand dune so that its head is lower than its back end and the water runs down its back into its mouth.

The Aporosaura lizard has a novel way of cooling off, by lifting up its back legs and tail and balancing on the hot sand like a tiny acrobat. The webbed feet of the palmato gecko allow it to scurry across soft sand rather than sink into it and tunnel into the dunes in day time to avoid the sun. A spider known as the 'dancing white lady' (because of its ritual display when threatened) constructs sand tunnels which are carefully lined with webbing to prevent cave-ins.

The gila monster and beaded lizard, the only poisonous lizards in the world, live in the south-western deserts of the USA. They feed on eggs, baby birds and the slower-moving rodents, and in times of plenty, their tails swell and grow longer as they store fat, which they use for survival when food is scarce. Their multi-coloured skins warn potential predators that they are poisonous, but if cornered

LEFT: *The spotted skunk keeps predators at bay by squirting a smelly liquid that can cause temporary blindness.*

they will sink their teeth into an opponent and simply hang on. Venom is produced in the lower jaw and this drips into the open wound.

Even though desert birds are shielded from the worst of the heat by their feathers, they still prefer to feed in early morning and evening, sheltering during the rest of the day. The gila woodpecker makes its home in the saguaro cactus of

Arizona and Mexico, the spines of which afford it protection from intruders. It hollows out a nest hole in the fleshy stem a year in advance so that the sap will harden into a protective shell around the hole. An abandoned nest often becomes home later to the small cactus wren or the sparrowhawk.

The sand grouse may be nesting 80 km (50 miles) from water, but it has a clever solution to the problem of providing its chicks with water. The male flies off to the nearest water hole where, as he drinks, he fluffs out his feathers until they are full of water. He then returns to the nest where the chicks gather under his top feathers to suck out the moisture. Sand grouse chicks are so programmed to this method of drinking that when they are raised in captivity they will only drink by sucking the moisture from some type of fabric.

The roadrunner, found in the stony deserts of North America, is a member of the cuckoo family, though it does not, like many species, lay its eggs in other birds' nests. It can fly, rather inefficiently, but it prefers to run from trouble and when pounding along on its powerful legs with wings outstretched, it can reach 24 km/h (15 mph). Its long tail can steer and brake, enabling it to change direction suddenly or come to an abrupt stop. It lives on insects, lizards and small snakes and can kill with a single stab of its sharp beak.

Desert cats

Even wild cats turn into burrowing animals in the desert, though the smallest of them, the black-footed cat of southern Africa, often takes over burrows vacated by hares, or camps in old termite nests. Despite the female's small size – she may weigh only 1.5 kg (3 lb) – she is a ferocious little creature, preying on squirrels, reptiles and birds. Females are 'on heat' for only a day or so, making loud mewing calls to attract a mate, and their kittens are born underground. The mother usually moves them soon after birth, as birth smells may attract predators to the nest. Kittens are born with pink pads and only develop the black markings that give the cat its name after about six weeks. They are very precocious, however, walking at two weeks and exploring beyond the nest a few days later.

The sand cat of the Sahara, with its soft,

dense, sandy-coloured fur and white muzzle with a reddish streak across the cheeks, has thick hair on its feet to dull the effect of the burning sand and to help it walk without sinking. It has strong legs to dig burrows and large, low-set ears to detect any movement of its prey at night. It eats rodents, lizards and birds and obtains the water it needs from their bodies. Litters may contain as many as seven or eight kittens, and though they are very small at birth, weighing about 39 g (1.4 oz), they will put on another 255 g (9 oz) within the next three weeks.

Working animals

The most familiar and visible desert animals are the camels, which have been used as working animals from the earliest times. The Arabian camel, or dromedary, is a native of the Middle East and North Africa, though only the domesticated strain exists today. It is slightly taller than the two-humped Bactrian camel, standing up to 2.4 m (8 ft) at the shoulder, but the Bactrian is stronger and more heavily built, making it a more useful pack animal. Domesticated Bactrians are found in Asia and the only remaining wild

camels live in the Gobi Desert.

The physiological make-up of the camel means that it is well suited to desert life. Its body temperature has a wide range, dropping at night and rising so slowly during the day that the animal will only sweat when it reaches 40°C (104°F).

ABOVE: *Although the roadrunner can fly, it prefers to run, reaching speeds of up to 24 km/h (15 mph).*

39

In addition, the camel's blood does not thicken as readily as that of other animals in response to heat and loss of moisture, and by concentrating its urine, it is able to conserve water. Its hump, though not a reserve of water as many people believe, is made up of fatty tissue which can provide energy when food is in short supply, and can weigh as much as 45 kg (99 lb). A camel can survive for a long time without drinking, then when water is available it can drink something like 100 l (22 gallons) in a matter of minutes. At such a time the camel will visibly swell as the water passes into the body tissues.

The camel's foot is divided into two halves joined by a web of skin and is protected by a tough padded sole so that the splayed feet can carry its weight across the sand without sinking. Its long, thick, double row of eyelashes keeps sand out of its eyes and, for the same purpose, it can close its nostrils. As it walks it has a swaying motion because both back and front feet on one side move at the same time.

RIGHT: *The camel walks with a swaying motion because both front and back feet on one side move at the same time.*

CHAPTER FOUR

The Polar Lands

At the far north and south of the earth, the frozen wastes around the poles are an impossible habitat for humans, but animals have found their own methods of survival. Antarctica is the world's coldest and most isolated continent, most of it permanently covered by an ice cap that is over 4 km (2.5 miles) thick in places. It cannot support animal life but the seas surrounding it are rich in food for penguins and seals, and in the spring, they come ashore to breed. In the Arctic, temperatures are well below freezing for most of the year, except for the brief summer period, when it is light for 24 hours a day. At this time, the snows of the treeless tundra melt, and animals can feed on mosses, lichens and stunted shrubs.

The most familiar animals of the Antarctic are probably the penguins; strutting about like stiff little men in dinner jackets. Penguins cannot fly but they are strong swimmers, their wings having evolved into powerful flippers which they use for propulsion, enabling them to 'fly' through the water. When swimming they can keep up a steady speed of 7–10 km/h (4–6 mph), and if necessary, they can go twice as fast in short bursts. A thick layer of protective blubber under the skin helps to keep them warm in the icy seas and their waterproof coats are made up of two layers of thick feathers to conserve body heat. Penguins are normally black with an white belly but many have distinctive crests or markings around the head. The

FACING PAGE: *These adelie penguins are kept warm in the icy seas by a thick layer of protective blubber under their skin.*

rockhopper has a red bill and a crest of yellow feathers, the emperor has a yellow and orange collar, and the chinstrap has a black line below the chin. Macaronis have a drooping orange crest and take their name from the eighteenth-century American dandies who wore feathers in their hats and were nicknamed 'macaronis'.

Penguin parents

Pairs of penguins usually mate for life and every year in the spring they return to the same nesting site or rookery to raise their young. Rookeries contain as many as a million birds and most are near the sea's food supply. Some, however, are a day's journey from the edge of the ice and the penguins will cover much of the distance by 'tobogganing' – sliding across ice and snow on their bellies, while pushing themselves along with feet and flippers.

All together there are seventeen species of penguins, and they usually build nests in rocks or clumps of grass. In the commonest species, the adelie, the male brings pebbles which the female arranges in a circle. In most species, males and females take turns minding the chicks and bringing fish and the females feed their offspring with partly digested food which the chicks take from inside their mouths. When the chicks are a few weeks old they gather in 'crèches', which may contain a hundred or more birds, huddling together for warmth while their parents go hunting for fish. When the adults return they call for their chicks who come waddling out of the crèche for their food.

The largest of the penguins, the emperor, has the strangest of breeding habits, as it 'nests' on an ice shelf where there are no nesting materials. The female lays her single egg in complete darkness, in temperatures as low as -25°C (-13°F) and carries it on her feet, covered with a layer of skin, because if it touched the ice it would not survive. A few days later the female passes the egg on to the male before leaving for the sea. It is then the male's turn to balance the egg on his feet, and he does this for the whole of the two-month incubation period, during which time he eats nothing. Not until the female returns with a supply of fish for the newly hatched chick can the male return to sea and eat to regain his lost weight.

44

RIGHT: *The largest of the penguin species, the emperor penguin 'nests' on a barren, icy shelf.*

ABOVE: *Elephant seal pups are weaned and able to fend for themselves about a month after birth.*

FACING PAGE: *The walrus uses its long tusks to dig for clams, and as a deterrent to would-be predators.*

Sleek and streamlined

The main enemy of the penguins is the leopard seal, which lives a solitary life on the fringes of the Antarctic pack ice. Named for its spotted coat, it feeds mainly on fish, but its powerful jaws can slice into a penguin and even swallow one of the smaller species whole. It often lurks near a rookery to pick off a bird as it dives into the sea. Like all the seals, this species is perfectly adapted for running down its prey in the water. The shape of the seal is sleek and streamlined and its four limbs are modified for speedy swimming, with the hind flippers providing the power and the front being used to steer. Under water it can close its nostrils to prevent water from getting into its lungs.

The most common type of seal is the crabeater seal, which, in spite of its name, feeds mainly on krill. Its upper and lower teeth fit together like a sieve to strain small fish from the water. There are so many crabeaters in the Antarctic that it is reckoned that they eat over 60 million tonnes of krill a year. They are seldom seen on land but in spring each pair breeds on a separate floe in the pack ice. The male will defend his territory vigorously against all comers. A different method of protecting its young is employed by the ringed seal, which uses its well-developed claws to scratch a lair in a ridge of ice.

The fur seal, so-called because of the heavy mane worn by the male around his neck and shoulders, and the elephant seal, recognizable by his trunk-like snout,

are both land-breeding seals, choosing the same stretch of beach every year. The males arrive first to stake out their territory and then, as the females flock in, the bulls try to shepherd as many as possible into their harem. The females are already pregnant from the previous year and give birth a few days after arrival. Soon afterwards they mate with the bulls, who will fight to retain their harems, rearing up and slashing at a rival with their sharp canines, sometimes inflicting deep wounds. The male elephant seal will inflate his trunk to make himself look bigger and let out a fearsome roar that can be heard for several kilometres. The elephant seal pup is weaned and ready to hunt for itself in about a month, as neither male nor female feeds while on shore. By contrast, the fur seal mothers stay with their pups for eight days, allowing them to suckle. Then they go to sea for three days before returning well fed, with their milk replenished and they continue with this pattern of three days ashore and three days at sea for about four months.

The noisy, sociable walrus, which gets its name from the Norse word for 'sea horse', is a cousin of the seal and can be seen, a hundred at a time, basking in the sun on an ice floe. When on land it can turn its hind flippers under its body so that it can pull itself along by all four limbs. The male is about a third larger than the female, weighing as much as 1,400 kg (3,000 lb), and though both sexes have long tusks, the female's are more slender. The walrus feeds on shellfish from the sea bed, using its tusks to dig for clams, then cracking open the shells with its teeth. Its sensitive moustache helps it to distinguish edible shellfish from stones. The male's tusks can be up to 76 cm (30 in) long and weigh as much as 4 kg (9 lb), making formidable weapons. Though a polar bear might seize a pup, given the opportunity, it would not tackle a full-grown walrus.

The great carnivore

The polar bear, among the largest of the world's carnivores, preys mainly on seals, as well as fish and seabirds, and it can hook a 225-kg (496-lb) seal out of the water with a single heave of its paw. The ringed seal is its particular favourite because of its breathing holes in the ice and its maternity lair, both of which the

FACING PAGE: *As winter sets in, polar bears travel south after spending the summer foraging in the Arctic.*

bear can scent as far away as 1 km (0.6 mile). It then waits patiently beside the breathing hole and seizes the seal's head in its jaws as it pop out, or it raids the lair during the six weeks the mother is nursing her pups. Its other methods of hunting are to swim underwater to the edge of an ice floe, then rear up suddenly to snatch a basking seal or, when stalking in the open, to flatten its head and shoulders on the ice and push itself slowly along by its back legs until it is within striking distance. Once it has made a kill, it skins the seal neatly, eating only the blubber and entrails, though if it is very hungry it may eat the whole carcass. After its meal it will clean it face and wash its coat, just like a cat.

The 'lord of the Arctic' is perfectly adapted for its life among the icy waters, its colour blending into the dazzling white background so that, in spite of its bulk, it is scarcely visible. Its thick, water-repellent coat has a dense underfur, and beneath its skin is a layer of fat up to 10 cm (4 in) thick, so that its body temperature can remain constant in temperatures as low as -37°C (-35°F). Its enormous feet act as snowshoes on the ice and like paddles in the water and have hairy soles to

ABOVE: *In winter, the stoat exchanges its reddish-brown summer coat for snow-white fur.*

prevent it from slipping on the ice.

In spite of its great bulk – the male can weigh up to 800 kg (1,764 lb) – the polar bear is very agile, being able to run at up to 50 km/h (35 mph) and swim for hundreds of kilometres. Its body can store a large amount of fat when plenty of prey is available to use when food is scarce. This is particularly important for the females, who retire to a maternity den in the snow for five or six months while they wean their cubs and do not emerge again until spring, when the cubs are old enough to follow their mothers on a long trek to a promising hunting ground.

Tundra dwellers

Through the winter months, the Arctic fox dogs the footsteps of the polar bear, feeding on the abandoned seal carcass when the bear moves on. Sometimes it will follow the bear far out across the ice, so that it is completely dependent on the bear's leftovers. Like the bear it has non-slip soles to its feet. Its winter coat is as white as the surrounding snow but in summer, when it preys mainly on the lemmings that feed on the low plants of the tundra, it is greyish-yellow, to blend better with the scenery. The number of foxes rises and falls along with the lemming population. Though the usual number of fox cubs in a litter is seven, in years when the lemmings are scarce this will fall to four or five and when the lemmings are plentiful, there may be as many as twenty.

The snowy owl population, too, depends to a large extent on the availability of lemmings. The female may lay up to fifteen eggs at a time, in a hollow in the ground, but many of the resulting owl chicks will starve if there are not enough lemmings to go round among the predators. The snowy owl is one of the world's hardiest birds, normally living on the tundra throughout the year. It has dense feathers on its legs and feet for warmth, large eyes for the day and night hunting and strong talons to seize its prey. Besides lemmings it hunts rabbits, hares and ducks and is good at catching fish, lying in wait beside the water, then pouncing with claws outstretched. Its plumage is white all year round with dark barred markings, which are more obvious in the female, to give her better camouflage as she sits motionless on the ground incubating her eggs.

RIGHT: *Living on the tundra all year round, the snowy owl is one of the world's hardiest birds.*

The stoat, like the fox, is one of the creatures that exchanges its reddish-brown summer coat for a white winter one. This has not been entirely to their advantage, as the white coat is ermine, which has been in great demand by the fur trade. Stoats are fast-running, powerful creatures with small, sharp eyes. They are voracious carnivores, hunting at night in family groups and preying mainly on birds, voles and, of course, the unfortunate lemming.

Lemmings, hamster-like animals measuring up to 15 cm (10 in) long, are the commonest animal found on the northern tundra. They feed on grass and small plants, and spend the winter in long winding tunnels under the snow. Every few years a population explosion occurs amongst the lemmings, so that their numbers outstrip the food supply, leading to a mass migration. Once the migration frenzy is under way millions of lemmings race across the tundra. If they reach the coast they will hurl themselves into the sea and keep swimming until they drown, which has led to the popular misconception that they organize a mass suicide.

Remarkable animals

Two of the most remarkable animals of the Arctic are the musk ox and the reindeer. The musk ox spends all year on the tundra, impervious to the icy blizzards because of its thick woolly undercoat topped by a shaggy mantle of long hair which reaches almost to the ground in winter. It weighs around 444 kg (882 lb), and lives on grass and shrubs in summer, while in winter it survives on lichens and the fat stored in its body. Musk oxen live in herds of between twenty and a hundred, huddling together for warmth, with the backs to the wind and when threatened by wolves the adults form a ring around their young to protect them. Their sideways curving horns will make any predatory wolf think twice about attacking.

The chief food of the reindeer is lichen, which is often called 'reindeer moss'. In summer the reindeer roam over the treeless tundra in herds, but in winter they travel long distances southwards to find food and shelter in the forests. They are expert at digging out food in the most barren of terrain; their sharp hooves can cut through all but the thickest ice and they use their large hooves for shovelling aside earth or snow to expose the lichens underneath. They are closely related to the North American caribou, which gets its name from the Indian word for 'shoveller'.

Reindeer are the only members of the deer family where both sexes have antlers, though the males shed theirs after the autumn mating season, while those of the female are shed in summer. They are also the only deer to have been domesticated, supplying milk, meat and skins for northern peoples just as cattle do in other areas, with the added bonus that they can provide a useful means of transport in the snow.

FACING PAGE: *Male reindeers shed their antlers after the mating season, while the females shed theirs in summer.*

52

CHAPTER FIVE

Woodland and Forest

The trees of our woodlands and forests, whether the broad-leaved varieties of the deciduous woodlands or the pines and firs of the cooler coniferous belts, provide food and a sheltered habitat for the rich variety of animals living in them or under them. There is a well-stocked larder of greens, berries, fruit and nuts as well as plenty of ready-made refuges and look-out posts.

Many species of deer roam the forests of Europe, the Americas, Asia and Africa, often clinging to the thickets by day and venturing out to feed in clearings in the late evening. Some are grazers and some are browsers, but all are ruminants – animals that chew the cud. Most male deer have branched antlers which are shed each year, then grow again from buds

that appear on the head, and are used to defend territory or do battle over females in the mating season. The handsome red deer, known as wapiti in North America, has antlers that can measure up to 1 m (3 ft) and weigh 9 kg (20 lb). It is found mainly in open woodland where it browses on leaves, but it is very adaptable and in some parts of the world it lives on open grassland or even in semi-desert. In the excitement of the rutting season the males wallow in mud and their bellowing carries for several kilometres.

The smallest of the European deer, the roe deer, standing only 65–75 cm (25–30 in) at the shoulder, barks like a dog in the rutting season, as well as when giving warning of danger. The bucks mark their territory by shredding the bark of trees

FACING PAGE: *The roe deer makes a distinctive barking sound during the rutting season or when warning other deer of danger.*

ABOVE: *During its six- or seven-month hibernation, the dormouse loses half its original body weight.*

FACING PAGE: *Instead of hibernating during winter, the badger lays down fat, more than doubling its 'summer weight'.*

of perfume. It has no antlers but the male has canine teeth 7 cm (3 in) long protruding from his mouth, and these are used for fighting. In the first quarter of this century, 10,000–15,000 of these animals were trapped and shot each year for their musk glands, resulting in their extinction in some of their original habitats. It is now possible, however, to extract musk without killing the deer and many are kept on special ranches in China for this purpose.

Night life

Much of the woodland life is nocturnal, for at night small animals can emerge to forage without fear of disturbance by humans. The secretive dormouse is widely distributed throughout the world but it is seldom seen. It is an agile climber and lives mainly in trees, feeding on nuts, fruit and seeds. Many build domed nests in shrubs or tree hollows by skilfully weaving together grass, leaves and bark, and in winter they hibernate, rolling into a ball and sleeping for six or seven months at a stretch. During hibernation their temperature drops and their heartbeat almost stops. When they wake in

with their antlers until the wood is exposed. They have only one mate and will defend her and their territory against any newcomers.

One of the most unusual species is the small musk deer of Asia, taking its name from the scent gland in front of the male's navel which, in the mating season, excretes a strong-smelling substance that is much sought-after for the manufacture

April or May, they will have lost half their original body weight.

The badger, another nocturnal denizen of the woods, does not hibernate but instead lays down fat under the skin so that it more than doubles its weight. It then spends a peaceful, fairly inactive winter living off its fat reserves below ground. It excavates its burrows, or sets, with its powerful front paws, making an extensive system of underground passages and chambers. One set may be occupied by one or two families, numbering up to fifteen animals, and may be used by successive generations. At night badgers come out to feed on worms, frogs and voles, as well as vegetables, returning to the set to sleep during the day. Visitors during the day may spot their presence only by the entrances to the set, which consist of several holes a few metres apart, measuring about 25 cm (10 in) in diameter, each with a pile of excavated earth in front. Badgers prefer to live in undisturbed woodland and usually stick to well-beaten paths between the set and the best feeding areas. The edges of their territory are usually defined by specially dug pits, which the badgers use as latrines.

Farm pests

Much the same size as the badger is the racoon which, with its black eye-patches, belongs to the same family as the panda. There are seven species in the racoon family, the most widespread being the North American racoon. The usual signs of its presence are its footprints on river banks, showing five long, unwebbed toes on each foot, and the scratches around the tree-hole it uses as a day-time nest. The racoon usually chooses a home near water and hibernates only in the northern US and Canada, where the winters are harsh. Though it climbs easily and is almost as much at home in the trees as a squirrel, it forages mainly on the ground. It has a wide taste in food which it seems to wash before eating: frogs and small rodents as well as nuts and fruit form a regular part of its diet. It has a particular liking for crayfish but will raid an orchard or a chicken coop whenever it has the chance, causing farmers to view it as a pest.

Another 'enemy' of the farmer is the wild boar. It forages over a wide area for food, and is not averse to raiding crops which grow near forests, particularly

FACING PAGE: *Although it will eat a wide variety of food (from nuts to crayfish), the racoon seems to wash everything before eating it.*

beetroot and potatoes. As sows and young boar live in herds of up to fifty, this can become a serious problem in some areas. This ancestor of the domestic pig has a similar thick-set body and short neck, but its legs are slightly longer and it has a long, tapering snout which it uses for rooting. It has a thick skin and a bristly coat, enabling it to crash through seemingly impenetrable thickets without harming itself. The male has tusks up to 30 cm (12 in) long; the lower canines curve upwards and the upper canines rub against them, honing them to razor-sharpness. These strong sharp tusks can inflict serious wounds if the boar is alarmed or challenged in any way.

The quills of the porcupine also make a formidable weapon. The animal will first rattle its quills at a predator, but if this does not work it will charge backwards, driving its detachable spines into its enemy. It needs this defence as the long curved claws which serve it well as burrowing tools make it difficult to run. Usually porcupines spend the day in caves or burrows but the species found in Canada and South America are tree-climbers – some even have prehensile bristled tails to help with climbing – and nest aloft.

They feed on fruit, berries and roots and cause a great deal of damage by gnawing at trees or scratching up crops.

Winter stores

Trees suffer even more from the attentions of the beaver. It feeds on the bark, shoots and leaves of trees such as birch, willow and aspen, and can fell trees up to 50 cm (19 in) in diameter, both to get at the food and to obtain branches for damming rivers. Though some beavers live in holes in the river bank, others dam the flow of rivers to make suitable ponds for their lodge construction.

Dams and lodges are both extraordinary feats of construction. Branches needed for the dam are first floated and then manoeuvred into position, before being woven together and weighed down with stones. Gaps in the dam are filled with a mixture of clay and dead leaves. The lodge is then built in much the same way and may be as high as 2 m (6 ft). It is entered from under water, where sloping passages lead to the central nesting chamber.

A pair of beavers spends six or eight weeks building the lodge in autumn and

FACING PAGE: *Using its strong incisor teeth as chisels, a beaver can fell a tree 12 cm (5 in) in diameter in less than thirty minutes.*

ABOVE: *Though red squirrels will forage on the forest floor, they will return to the treetops before eating.*

tails on the water, whereupon all the beavers in the area will dive for cover.

Like the beaver, the red squirrel lays down stocks for the winter, hiding nuts and acorns in underground stores which it can locate by smell, even when they are well covered by snow. It also stores fat in its body. It favours heavily forested areas with pine, spruce and larch trees which can provide year-round food. After a good year, when plenty of hazelnuts and pine cones are available, the squirrel population will increase as they survive the winter in good condition and breed easily. In a poor year, when their reserves of fat are insufficient, many adult squirrels will die and far fewer babies will be reared.

Though squirrels will forage on the ground for food, they usually carry it back up the tree before eating it, sitting up on their hind legs, their bushy tails helping them to balance on a branch. Their long, sharp claws, combined with their ability to grip with their toes, equip them perfectly for life in the trees, and they are even able to scurry down a tree trunk head first. They also make long leaps from tree to tree, spreading their legs and using their tails for balance.

stocking it with wood, creating a warm and safe environment in which to spend the winter. Once the ice has broken, in spring, the beavers will emerge to cut down a few more trees. Their thick fur is water-repellent and the webbing on their feet and their powerful tails make them strong swimmers. They rely on their acute hearing to detect danger and will warn their fellows by slapping their flat

Stealthy hunters

The wolf has perhaps the worst reputation of the forest dwellers. This fearsome reputation is rather undeserved, however, as it is extremely unlikely that it would attack a human being unless cornered. In fact, the wolf has far more reason to fear us than the other way round. At one time, the grey or timber wolf was common throughout Europe, North America and Asia, but its numbers have been cut drastically. In North America it has almost been exterminated, and elsewhere it is confined to the wilder, less inhabited forests of the north. It is, however, an awesome predator, hunting in packs made up of one or two families, who co-operate to bring down a large animal such as an elk. It is a strong enough swimmer to hunt and kill a deer if it takes to the water, and it has enough stamina to outrun its prey, combined with the ability to reach 65 km/h (40 mph) over short distances. Though it lunges for the hind legs of prey on the run, the killing bite is delivered to the throat.

The wolf is the largest member of the dog family and looks a little like a German shepherd dog, though it has a

larger muzzle and stronger jaws. It is intelligent and cunning and has many of the characteristic reactions of the domestic dog: wagging its tail in greeting, lowering its tail between its legs in submission, and laying back its ears and drawing up its lips as it prepares to attack.

The lynx and the smaller but equally fierce bobcat are also clever hunters but

ABOVE: *The wolf is a cunning predator, working in packs to bring down large animals such as elk.*

they rely on strength rather than speed, prowling silently along the ground or lying in wait for their prey and pouncing from a rock or low branch. Their normal diet is hares, rodents and birds but they can also take a deer by leaping on to its back. When food is scarce they will attack domestic animals such as sheep or goats. Both belong to the same branch of the cat family and are distinguished by their short tails and ears surmounted by pointed tufts. These tufts are particularly long in the lynx, and it is thought that they may help to channel sounds and so increase their excellent hearing.

Bear refuge

The brown bear is the commonest of the bears, found in the forests of Europe, Asia and North America. In the past it inhabited the wide open spaces but fear of hunters caused it to seek refuge among the trees, and now it usually haunts the least accessible parts of the forest. In Europe, bears have been hunted so vigorously that they are wary and elusive creatures, but in North America they are bolder, scavenging in campsites and sometimes attacking humans. Brown bears are sturdy animals weighing any-thing up to 100 kg (220 lb) and when they stand on their hind legs, such as when investigating a strange sound or catching a scent, they reach 1.5–2.5 m (5–8 ft). Though they normally move slowly, they can run quite fast when nec-essary; they swim well and can climb trees, helped by their long, curved claws.

An adult bear needs some 10 kg (22 lb) of food a day and its main diet consists of roots, leaves, grass and fruit. It will also raid wild hives for honey, dig out anthills to eat the occupants, and fish for salmon. It is an amazing sight to witness several dozen bears gathered in a salmon stream at spawning time, busily flipping fish from the water with their paws.

By the first snowfall, the bear will have retreated to its winter den where it will hibernate for five to seven months. Though it does not sleep throughout the period, it will not eat again until spring. Cubs are born during hibernation, but these are entirely the responsibility of the females. Apart from the mating time, the male is a solitary animal and he does not join the female in hibernation. The cubs are born blind and helpless, weighing only about 680 g (24 oz). When there are

two in a family, there is usually one of each sex. They stay with their mother for three years, so females produce cubs only once in three or four years. Sometimes a young female from the last litter will stay to help look after the new cubs for the first few months.

ABOVE: *Brown bears are keen anglers; they will wade into a salmon stream at spawning time and deftly flip fish on to the shore.*
FACING PAGE: *The bobcat relies on stealth, strength and surprise to catch its prey, often pouncing from a rock or low-hanging branch.*

Eucalyptus forests

In Australia, the 500 species of eucalyptus tree dominate 95 per cent of the forests. The long flat leaves of these evergreens, impregnated with aromatic oils, are poisonous to most animals but some, such as the koala and the possum, have digestive systems which can detoxify the leaves. The koala's extra-long intestine helps in this digestive process enabling it to feed from twelve species of eucalyptus. It eats around 1 kg (2.2 lb) of leaves a day, storing them in its cheek pouches. Its name comes from an Aboriginal word meaning 'no drink', for the koala obtains all the liquid it needs from the eucalyptus. It is happiest in the trees, seldom descending to the ground, sleeping in a comfortable fork by day and at night scaling the topmost branches in search of the tender new shoots. Though it is heavily built, weighing 5–8 kg (11–17 lb), it is a skilful climber, having one toe on each foot opposed to the rest, giving it the extra

Left: Though it does not look particularly graceful, the koala is a skilful climber and seldom leaves the treetops.

grip necessary to scale even smooth tree trunks. The female carries her baby, or sometimes twins, in her pouch for six months, after which time it clings to her back, where it will hang on during her next mating. At the turn of the century there were millions of koalas, but many have since been killed for their fur. Forest clearances have further reduced their numbers so that they are now scarce.

The possums were originally rainforest creatures but as rainforests declined and eucalyptus took over, many were able to adapt and take advantage of the more plentiful food supply offered by the sugary sap of the eucalyptus trees. Some possums developed the ability to glide, useful in these more open forests, made possible by the existence of supple membranes extending between their fore and hind limbs. The largest is the great glider, also called a 'flying frying pan', which can cover 91 m (100 yd) with ease as it glides from one tree to another.

The fluffy glider lives in groups of half a dozen, defending a territory of a dozen or so trees. It lands on the bark on all fours, often with its head downward, then slices into the bark with its teeth and spends several hours licking up the sap.

LEFT: *The honey possum uses its rough tongue to lap up nectar and pollen, mainly from eucalyptus and banksia flowers.*

Another glider, the sugar glider, also feeds on the sap of acacia trees, which is unpalatable to other possums, and obtains its protein by eating insects and butterfly larvae.

The ringtail possum, unlike other possum species, builds its own nest out of leaves and twigs rather than sheltering in tree forks, enabling it to live in immature woodlands. It has a prehensile tail which it uses as a climbing aid. The honey possum differs from its relatives in only feeding on nectar and pollen, mainly from eucalyptus and banksia flowers. It has no teeth but its brushtipped tongue extends 2.5 cm (1 in) beyond its nose, allowing it to reach deep into the flowers to gather up the food.

CHAPTER SIX

Animals in Danger

The pace of destruction of age-old wildlife habitats this century has been without precedent. Every year 100,000 square kilometres (39,000 square miles) of tropical forest are destroyed, and at this rate these forests, home to thousands of species of mammals, insects and birds, will have disappeared completely by the year 2025. As the developing countries struggle to feed their growing populations, forests of all types are cut down for timber or to make way for roads and towns, wetlands are drained, and grasslands are ploughed up for agriculture, leaving wild creatures with ever-diminishing habitats in which to survive.

Loss of habitat

In the Virunga range of extinct volcanoes along the borders of Zaire, Rwanda and Uganda, the mountain gorillas inhabit their last remaining forests, protected by government order in special reserves, though poachers still manage to elude the rangers and occasionally kill an animal to supply an unscrupulous trade in souvenir heads and hands. In recent years the Rwandan government has been successful in setting up schemes to allow tourists to visit the gorillas without disturbing them too much, thus bringing valuable foreign currency into the country and helping to convince the local people that it is desirable to preserve the forests rather than clearing them to create more land for cultivating crops. However, when civil war broke out in the spring of 1994, international conservationists were forced to leave and it may be a long time before the effect on the gorilla population can be measured.

FACING PAGE: *Despite government protection, gorillas are still sometimes killed by poachers supplying the trade in souvenir heads and hands.*

ABOVE: *With its thin, long middle finger, the aye-aye scrapes out the inside of sugar cane and digs out insects from tree bark.*

FACING PAGE: *The biggest threat to the panda is from humans, who have cleared the bamboo forests on which pandas feed.*

The strangest of the primates, the aye-aye, is on the brink of extinction, clinging on to the remnants of its habitat left by the slash-and-burn methods of agriculture on the island of Madagascar. This odd little creature, with its big round ears and staring eyes, spends its days in nests built high in the trees, emerging at night to crunch noisily on fruits or coconuts. It has an elongated middle finger, as thin as a wire, which it uses to scrape out the inside of sugar cane or to dig insects from the bark of trees. Some local tribes believe that this third finger can be dried and used as a magic charm. Others believe that killing an aye-aye wards off bad luck, and yet others see them as vermin who raid coconut plantations and sugar cane groves. Given all these problems, perhaps the most remarkable thing about the aye-aye is that it has survived at all.

The giant panda, with the big 'teddy-bear' head, gentle face and black eye-patches, is a fitting symbol for the World Wide Fund for Nature (WWF), one of the world's leading conservation organizations. Representing all the rare and endangered animals that need strict protection in order to survive, the WWF has an extremely important task before it.

The pandas are found only in the remote mountain areas of south-west China among the bamboo forests that provide their food. Once they were far more numerous and widespread but many were killed for their skins or captured for zoos. However, the major threat to the species has been the destruction of its habitat by humans.

Almost the entire diet of the giant panda comes from the shoots and leaves of some thirty species of bamboo. The male panda can weigh as much as 130 kg (286 lb) and will spend twelve to fourteen hours a day feeding, munching its way through 15 kg (33 lb) of food. The best and most succulent stands of bamboo have been cut down to make way for farmland so there is less food available and panda numbers have fallen accordingly. They are now limited to pockets of bamboo in six small areas, which has led to in-breeding within the limited community and inevitable weakening of the stock. Natural disasters can occur occasionally if all the bamboo in a particular area flowers at the same time, so that later in the season it all dies back at once. In the past, pandas would simply have moved to another forest but now this is

71

no longer possible and there have been instances when a number have died of starvation.

By the 1980s it was estimated that there were only a thousand or so giant pandas left in the world. There have been rigorous efforts to increase the captive population, including the famous attempts in Moscow and London to persuade their pandas An-An and Chi-Chi to mate. Expensive breeding programmes, with trials of artificial insemination, have had scant success, with only two or three cubs born a year. Unfortunately, the majority fail to survive beyond six months.

The animal trade

Many species have been hunted almost out of existence by those who trade in animal products, be it meat, fur or skin. The fashion for crocodile or alligator handbags and shoes led to the shooting of countless numbers of our largest reptiles. By 1930, nearly 200,000 Florida alligators

RIGHT: *Fashion victims – alligators were almost wiped out by the trade in alligator shoes and handbags, before becoming a protected species.*

72

were being killed in a year. Thirteen years later they were scarce enough for the price on their heads to have increased ten-fold and yet hunters still managed to take under 7,000. Since 1943 they have been protected and they can now easily be seen gliding through the swamps or basking in the sun.

A full-length coat made from the fur of the snow leopard would cost the lives of four adult animals and sell for more than $30,000 on the Western black market. Such a trade is, of course, illegal as the snow leopard has been a protected species since 1983, but there are still poachers willing to supply it. This magnificent animal, with its heavy, frosty-grey coat patterned with dark rosettes, is solitary and little known. It haunts the remote, icy mountain regions of central Asia just below the permanent snow line, preying on blue sheep, wild boar, deer and ibex. Its favourite method of hunting is to stalk its prey from above, dropping down when least expected, being strong and brave enough to bring down an animal twice its own weight. It will also raid domestic sheep and cattle, which brings it into conflict with local farmers.

The world-wide population of snow leopards is thought to be about 5,000, but with such an elusive animal this can only be guesswork. Only its wariness, and the inaccessibility of its mountain home, have saved it from extinction.

Whaling slaughter

Whales have been hunted for thousands of years, but not until the mid-nineteenth century had it become a profitable international business. As well as the meat they had always provided, their oil was much in demand for fuel and their bones for women's corsets. The exploding harpoon was invented for efficient killing and great factory ships extracted the oil from the whale carcass while still at sea. From the 1930s to the 1950s, though the need for fuel oil and whalebone had disappeared, whales were still being slaughtered for their flesh at the rate of 30,000 a year. As one species declined so that it was no longer worth hunting, another became the target. Even after international regulations were imposed and the rare species were supposedly protected, some countries – chiefly those where whale meat is regularly eaten – continued to hunt and there is still an extremely

RIGHT: *Because it is so elusive, the snow leopard has managed to escape extinction at the hands of poachers.*

lucrative trade for whale meat in Japan, where it is regarded as an expensive delicacy.

The blue whale is the largest living animal, measuring some 300 m (100 ft) and weighing as much as 100 tonnes. Once it was found in all oceans but its size made it a great prize for whalers. In 1980 it was calculated that there were perhaps only 8,000 left. The grey whale had already disappeared from the Atlantic by the late eighteenth century. One hundred years later it had all but vanished from the East Pacific and was almost hunted to extinction in the West Pacific by the mid-1960s, though since protection its numbers have increased again. Right whales, recognizable by the patches of barnacles and crustaceans around their enormous heads, were so-called because hunters considered them the 'right' whales to catch and they are now rare. The blue, grey and right whales are all baleen whales; they live on krill and have horny plates in their mouths instead of teeth,

Left: Killer whales live together in packs, or 'pods', of twenty to fifty individuals, and communicate using whistles, clicks and calls.

with fringes of bristle which strain the food from the water.

The toothed whales include the sperm whale, which has been extensively hunted since the early eighteenth century, and the killer whale, with its distinctive black-and-white markings which are familiar to visitors to aquaria throughout the world. Killer whales are intelligent and easily trained, so they have been much in demand for display; however, there is now a strong body of opinion which is opposed to keeping them in captivity. Though they are not officially an endangered species, many have been killed because they compete with fishermen for fish stocks, and they are subject to local exploitation in many regions.

All whales, in common with all marine life, are in danger from the millions of gallons of industrial waste poured into the seas each year, polluting the water and poisoning their feeding grounds. Another threat comes from the nylon nets used for commercial fishing: whales often

RIGHT: *The black rhino is threatened with extinction because its horn is used in Oriental medicines.*